Dear reader

The postal addresses used in this book have all been changed to fictitious places. The email addresses have also been censored. All the photographs are posed by models.

The girls are taller than me

Birstonable
NSW 2055

10 May

14 Dean Street
Hanford
NSW 5321

Dear Jaleel

How are you? Do you remember how I told you about being small? Well, now you'll laugh. Remember Laura – that girl in my class who came to my party? We used to be the same height, but now she is much taller than me. So are most of her friends. I'm probably the youngest-looking boy in my class but it really bugs me when she says I'm a late developer. She thinks she's so grown up. I don't know what 'grown up' means anyway!

See you next month for football in the park!

Matt

Laura's diary

12 May
We had swimming today. I hate anyone seeing me in my costume. The boys were laughing and I'm sure they noticed that one of my breasts is a bit bigger than the other one. It's so embarrassing. I wish I was normal.

PROBLEM PAGE

ME AND MY BODY

JUDITH ANDERSON

W

FRANKLIN WATTS
LONDON • SYDNEY

Problem Page
Me and my body

Asking questions about your health is important, but it's not always easy – especially when it's an embarrassing problem! The letters and emails in this book are all from young people who have chosen to write, email or even text their problems to friends, or to an advice column. A few have only told their diaries…

The Facts

Growth spurts

✳ Girls have a rapid growth spurt between 11 and 13 years old. Boys have their growth spurt later, usually between 13 and 15 years old.

✳ Boys and girls start puberty at around the same time. However, boys' growth spurts come at the end of puberty, while girls have theirs at the beginning. This means that boys have a longer period of overall growth.

✳ Growth spurts begin with the hands and feet. Legs and arms come next, while a boy's chest and shoulders may not be fully developed until he is about 20 years old.

✳ Boys' and girls' bodies may develop unevenly to begin with. It is normal for one breast or one testicle to be larger than the other at first. After a few months, they usually even out.

What's normal?

I can't wait to get a bra. My best friend has been wearing one for months.
Paula, aged 11

I don't think size has anything to do with maturity. My brother is over 182 cm tall but his behaviour is really immature!
Sophie, aged 12

I suppose we all just want to be the same as our friends, but I don't think there is such a thing as a completely average person.
Ben, aged 13

Your Views

How do you think Matt and Laura should deal with their worries? What does 'grown up' mean to you?

I don't want periods

Summerplace
SR2 9OG

29 April

Rachel Says Letters Page
My Life Magazine
327 Canning Road
High Town H53 7YG

Dear Rachel

My periods started a couple of months ago. I thought it would be okay but it's not. I had my second period six weeks after my first, and now I have started again after only three weeks. My mum says it takes a while for periods to become regular, but how will I know when the next one is going to start?

Another problem is that I don't feel very well. My stomach hurts and my legs and back ache. I don't want to go to school but if I stay at home then my teacher might find out that I've got my period. I don't want anyone to know.

Claire (aged 13)

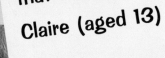

Rachel Says Letters Page
My Life Magazine
327 Canning Road
High Town H53 7YG

5 May

139 Prince's Street
Summerplace
SR2 9OG

Dear Claire

It does take a while for periods to settle down. Most girls find they begin to have a regular pattern after about a year. However, even though we talk about 'monthly' periods, your pattern may mean a period as often as every three weeks or as little as every five or six weeks. This is normal.

Many girls have some mild period pain. If your tummy aches try putting a hot water bottle on it. However, if you are worried about anything or if you feel really unwell don't keep it to yourself – tell someone like your mum or your doctor.

Rachel, Agony Aunt

Your Views

Do you think Claire should take the day off school?

The Facts
Periods

❋ During puberty a girl's uterus develops a lining of tissue and blood which it discards each month unless she is pregnant. This lining passes out of the vagina as menstrual blood – a period. The bleeding usually lasts for 4–7 days.

❋ Periods can start at any time from age 9 to 15 or even earlier or later.

❋ Some girls feel tired or faint during their periods. They may be lacking iron in their diets. Red meat and leafy green vegetables are good sources of iron.

❋ Most girls lose a total of 2–3 tablespoons of blood during each period. It isn't much but it often looks more!

❋ Period pain is caused by muscle cramps in your uterus, or womb. The good news is that many girls stop having bad period pain as they get older.

❋ Periods are a sign that a girl's body is healthy and working properly.

He smells terrible

From: kathrinep@~~██████████~~

To: zoe@~~█████~~.com

Date: Wednesday, November 19

Subject: What a pong!

Hi Zoe

Guess what?! I had to sit next to Aaron on the bus home! I tried not to breathe all the way but he really stinks! Hasn't he heard of washing, or deodorant, or putting on a clean shirt? I mean, we all get a bit sweaty sometimes, but Aaron has really bad BO. Why doesn't he do something about it? I think someone should tell him.

See you tomorrow :-).

Kate xx

Aaron's diary

19 November
I didn't want to take my coat off at school this morning. I know the girls think I'm disgusting. I could see them pulling faces when I walked into the classroom. I had a shower last night and another one after breakfast but that made me late and by the time I'd run for the bus I was soaked in sweat. Worrying about it just makes me sweat even more. I don't think it helps that I don't always have clean clothes to wear. Mum is always so busy. She says I should use the washing machine myself.

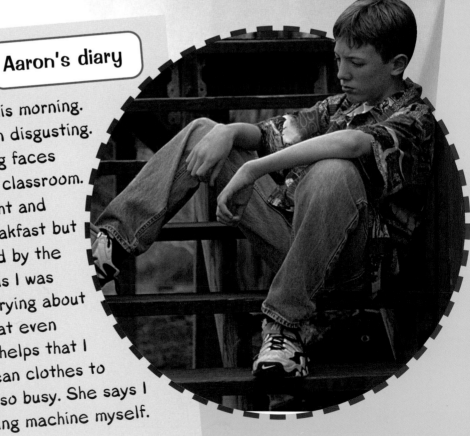

Top Tips
Get fresh

★ Body odour, or BO, is often triggered by puberty. Sweat in our armpits and groin area becomes very attractive to bacteria, which produce the bad smell. Regular washing is therefore very important.

★ Use an anti-perspirant to reduce sweating, and a deodorant to disguise the smell.

★ Wear fresh clothes each day. Clothes made of natural fibres are best. Cotton can be washed at a high temperature, which kills lingering bacteria. It also allows air to circulate more freely, and draws sweat away from your skin.

★ Avoid spicy foods and onions. These are known to increase your chances of BO.

★ If your feet are the problem, wear cotton socks or go without socks in the summer and avoid sweaty trainers. Always dry your feet carefully and use an anti-fungal powder.

How do you beat BO?

My sister says my bedroom smells bad in the mornings, so now I keep a window open at night.

Kieran, aged 12

I used to wear really perfumed deodorant. Now I go for something more neutral. It works just as well and it is less obvious.

Meg, aged 14

My dad won't let me watch TV until I've taken off my shoes and washed my feet!

Dom, aged 13

Your Views

Would you tell someone if they had really bad BO? Would you want a friend to tell you? What should Aaron do?

I hate pimples!

From: david.andrews@e~~verything~~~~gm~~il.com
To: rick521@b~~roadview~~~~.com~~
Date: Monday, April 21
Subject: Pimples

Hi Rick

How are you? Have you got any pimples yet? I've got loads on my forehead. BIG lumpy red ones :-(. My sister reckons squeezing them gets the bad stuff out, but when I tried it really hurt and now they look worse than ever. My friend's dad has lots of scars on his face from when he had zits, and I'm worried that I might end up looking the same. Mum says I shouldn't eat so much chocolate because it's bad for my skin, but no chocolate is almost as bad as having zits in the first place.

I'm supposed to be going bowling tonight with Liz and her mates, but I might spend my money on some zit cream instead. I don't want anyone seeing me like this.

David

From: david.andrews@e~~verything~~~~gma~~il.com
To: rick521@b~~roadview~~~~.com~~
Date: Monday, April 21
Subject: Re: Pimples

Hi Zit Face!

Send me a photo – I could do with a laugh! Bet you look a sight. Mind you, there are loads of kids in my class with zits so you're probably not on your own. Just go bowling and forget about it!

Rick

The Facts
Pimples

✻ Pimples are caused by a build-up of oil, or sebum, that blocks the tiny holes in our skin. Bacteria may become trapped, producing toxic chemicals that make the skin red and lumpy. Blackheads are pimples without the bacteria.

✻ Anyone can get pimples, but teenagers get more than their fair share because puberty triggers the production of too much sebum.

✻ Pimples are not caused by dirty skin, or by eating junk food. They come from sebum that is produced inside the skin.

✻ Acne is the name given to a heavy dose of red lumpy spots. Your doctor can treat it with anti-bacterial creams and other medication.

Top Tips
Living with pimples

★ Don't pick your zits – particularly the red lumpy sort. The bacteria will spread and you may end up with a scar.

★ Wash your skin twice a day but don't scrub it – scrubbing makes your skin produce more oil.

★ Keep oily make-up off your skin as it will only trap more bacteria.

★ Try to eat lots of fresh fruit and vegetables. The vitamins and minerals they contain help your skin to look its best. Drink lots of water too.

★ Remember that you are not the only person with zits! 80% of teenagers get them at some point.

Your Views

Should David spend his money on pimple cream, or go out with his friends?

I'm too tired

Top Tips

A good night's sleep

Changing sleep patterns are normal during puberty, but most 12-year-olds still need over nine hours sleep each night. Try these tips if you feel tired:

★ Don't watch TV or play computer games at night. They stimulate your brain and make it difficult to fall asleep.

★ Get plenty of exercise. You will find it easier to relax and sleep at bedtime.

★ If you are sleepy at school, try eating a healthy breakfast of cereal and milk or fruit juice. A quick snack won't keep you going through the morning. Your brain needs fuel to stay alert.

★ Don't worry if you have the occasional sleepless night. Talk your parents into letting you sleep in at the weekend.

What helps you to sleep?

I like staying up late at weekends. I just sleep until lunchtime the next day!

Sarah, aged 14

I know I'm really moody when I'm tired. If I can't sleep I think of something like my birthday party when I was a little kid. It's stupid, but it works.

Ali, aged 12

I always read a few pages of my book at night. It helps me to relax and fall asleep.

Tammy, aged 12

Your Views

What might be worrying Tina? What stops you from sleeping?

I just want to be thin

From: kylie_hynes@~~hydeandmorra.com~~

To: jules_agonyaunt@~~agonyaunt.com~~

Date: Friday, December 4

Subject: How can I make myself thin?

Dear Jules

I want to be a model when I'm older, but I know you have to be really thin and my thighs are too fat. I hate them. My cousin Fiona has long slim legs and I really want to be like her. I've been on a diet for the last two months but it doesn't seem to be working. Fiona says you have to exercise as well as diet but I get really tired when we do sport at school. What else can I do to make myself thin?

Kylie (12)

Kylie's diary

5 December

I skipped breakfast again this morning. I told Dad I'd eaten three pieces of toast! Altogether today I've had four crackers, an apple and a can of diet cola. I've still got supper to come, but we're having salad so it won't be too bad.

The Facts

Dieting

* A healthy diet does not necessarily mean cutting out food; it means eating the right kinds of food.

* Your growing body needs protein, found in fish, meat, cheese and eggs. It also needs calcium, found in dairy products like milk and yoghurt. Without these your muscles, nerves and skeleton cannot develop properly.

* Some people think they are fat, even when they are not. Sometimes they diet too much, depriving their bodies of vital food. This can lead to a serious illness called anorexia.

* People with anorexia often have a very low sense of their own worth. They need to eat, but they also need the support of family and friends if they are to get well.

From: jules_agonyaunt@~~████████~~
To: kylie_hynes@~~████████~~
Date: Monday, December 7
Subject: Re: How can I make myself thin?

Dear Kylie

I am really concerned by your email! When you are going through puberty your body grows and changes a lot. Your hips start to broaden and you may find that you are putting on some extra weight. This kind of change is not about being fat! It is about developing into a healthy woman.

Everyone has their own unique shape, and most girls do not have the thin legs of a catwalk model. No amount of dieting or exercise is going to change this, and in fact too much dieting can cause other problems. If you are too tired to take part in sport, it may be because you are not eating properly. Eating regular, balanced meals is one way to ensure that you look and feel your best.

Finally, and most important of all, try to focus on what you like about yourself. Smile when you next look in the mirror. It's a great way to feel good.

Jules, Agony Aunt

Your Views

Why does Kylie lie about eating to her dad? What would you do if you thought one of your friends wasn't eating enough?

17

The Facts

Smoking

❋ The tobacco in cigarettes contains nicotine. Nicotine is an addictive drug, which means that smokers find it difficult to be without it.

❋ Young people can become addicted to nicotine very quickly. You do not have to smoke many cigarettes before your body starts craving the drug.

❋ As many as two-thirds of all teenage smokers are addicted to nicotine. If they cannot stop smoking they have a 50% chance of developing lung cancer or heart disease later in life.

❋ The good news is that if you are able to quit smoking, you undo almost all the damage to your health.

❋ If you don't want to smoke but someone is putting pressure on you, practise saying no in front of the mirror, or make up an excuse like having a sore throat.

Why smoke?

All my friends smoke. They said they wouldn't let me be mates if I didn't smoke too.
Sanjet, aged 13

Some people say it's cool to smoke. I'm not sure. Why is it cool to cough out a cloud of smoke?
Sophie, aged 9

Smoking is great – it helps me relax.
Jackie, aged 14

My brother smokes. His breath stinks.
Darren, aged 12

Smoking costs a fortune. I'd rather spend my money on CDs.
Ryan, aged 12

Your Views

Why do you think Neil wants to try a cigarette? What would you say if your friend wanted you to smoke?

19

She's so overweight

21 Ballard Street
Instubbs TR2 9YT

10 July

Rachel Says Letters Page
My Life Magazine
327 Canning Road
High Town H53 7YG

Dear Rachel

My friend Natasha is very overweight. I think it's because she eats too much junk food. I've tried telling her to cut out the chips and chocolate but she says it is too hard. I know she hates being so big though. I went shopping with her on Saturday and when we were in the changing rooms she got really down about not being able to fit into any of the jeans.

Natasha is my best friend and I wish I could help her. Isn't it dangerous to be very overweight?

Grace (12)

Rachel Says Letters Page
My Life Magazine
327 Canning Road
High Town H53 7YG

12 July

21 Ballard Street
Instubbs TR2 9YT

Dear Grace

You are right to think that Natasha's weight may be caused by junk food. Foods like chips and chocolate contain lots of fat and sugar, which we know are 'fattening' foods. Also they do not contain much protein, fibre, or the vitamins and minerals we need to grow and to be healthy.

However, Natasha already knows that lots of sweets and crisps are bad for her. For some people, dealing with a weight problem is about more than just going on a diet. One way to help is to build up her confidence. Don't make her feel guilty about eating junk food, but encourage her to eat healthier foods. Exercise will also help. Is there a sport you could do with her?

If Natasha is very overweight (obese) she needs to see a doctor. She may be at risk from heart disease and other problems.

Rachel, Agony Aunt
PS I've attached a leaflet with some more information about healthy eating.

Rachel's factsheet: Eat well, stay well

*   The best way to achieve a healthy weight is to eat a varied diet of fresh food and to exercise regularly.

*   Eat lots of fruit and vegetables – about five portions a day.

*   Don't have sugary drinks and snacks too often. Drink more water.

*   Eat lots of high-fibre foods like jacket potatoes, rice, beans and cereals.

*   Watch out for processed foods like ready-meals and takeaways – they contain lots of sugar and fat.

*   Don't starve yourself – it isn't fun or healthy.

Your Views

Do you think it matters if someone is overweight?

I'm fed up with asthma

From: sam@~~spencerfamily~~y.com
To: yun-jae@~~shooptacht~~com
Date: Wednesday, October 14
Subject: Yesterday

Hi Yun-Jae

Thanks for coming over yesterday. I was pretty fed up after my asthma clinic appointment. The nurse went on and on about always having my inhaler with me and I ended up feeling really frightened.

My teachers at school know what to do if I can't breathe, but my friends don't. I suppose I should tell them but I hate everyone thinking there's something wrong with me. How do you deal with your peanut allergy?

Sam

From: yun-jae@~~shooptacht~~.com
To: sam@~~spencerfamily~~y.com
Date: Wednesday, October 14
Subject: Re: Yesterday

Hi Sam!

I could see you were fed up yesterday. In some ways it is easier for me because I know I won't have an allergic reaction if I don't eat anything with peanuts in. I do get worried when I go to a friend's house in case they forget to be careful, but I always carry my medicine, and I tell people about it in case of an emergency. It is important that everyone knows about my allergy. Don't worry about telling your friends, they will understand.

Yun-Jae

The Facts

Asthma and allergies

✳ Asthma is when a person's breathing airways are inflamed. Certain things like pets, tobacco smoke or house dust may irritate the airways and trigger an asthma attack, which is when it becomes harder to breathe.

✳ An allergy is when the body reacts strongly to a particular substance like peanuts or a bee sting or dairy products. Allergies can cause sickness, swellings or breathing problems. People with severe allergies may need emergency treatment.

✳ Asthma attacks and allergic reactions can be very frightening, but they can be treated with drugs given by a doctor.

✳ Some children find that their asthma or allergy becomes less severe as they get older.

Top Tips

Coping with your condition

⭐ Tell people about your asthma or allergy so that they know what to do if you become ill.

⭐ It is a good idea to wear a special bracelet or necklace containing details of your asthma or allergy. Your doctor will know where you can get one.

⭐ People with asthma or an allergy are not ill unless they are having an attack. If you keep your medicine with you and follow your doctor's advice, you can do almost anything you want.

Your Views

Why do you think Sam is reluctant to tell his friends about his asthma?

I can't remember what happened

Rachel Says Letters Page
My Life Magazine
327 Canning Road
High Town H53 7YG

Wintertree TR41 3IY

30 July

Dear Rachel

I thought I was okay with alcohol, but the other evening I got really drunk at a friend's party. There were loads of fruit drinks with vodka in them – three maybe. They didn't taste strong but I remember feeling dizzy and I know I threw up when I got home. The trouble is, I can't remember getting home. I've no idea if I walked or if someone gave me a ride.

Lots of my friends drink. Even my parents drink so I know it can't be that bad for you. So why did a few vodka drinks have such a big effect on me?

Stella (aged 13)

What do you think of alcohol?

> Drinking alcohol makes me feel less nervous at parties.
>
> Sam, aged 14

> Alcohol is full of calories - it's really fattening!
>
> Tanya, aged 15

> I like the names of alcopops, and I think the bottles look really cool.
>
> Mel, aged 14

> I hate the thought of losing control. What if I hurt myself, or said something stupid? I'd die of embarrassment.
>
> Charlie, aged 12

Your Views

Do you think it is okay to drink alcohol? Is there such a thing as a 'safe' amount?

Dear Stella

I'm glad you are concerned because being drunk is no joke! Alcohol is addictive, which means that we may become dependent on it and feel bad when we don't have it. It is also a depressant, which means that it slows down the way our bodies work.

Too much alcohol makes your body lose water (dehydrate), which gives you a 'hangover'. It may also make you lose control and affect your memory. But measuring the amount of alcohol in each drink can be tricky. 'Alcopops' are stronger than beer, but because they taste sweet it is easy to forget this.

So, next time you are at a party, be careful! Drink slowly and be aware of how it affects you. Drink glasses of water between alcoholic drinks so your body does not dehydrate. Try to eat as well – alcohol affects you more quickly on an empty stomach. Finally, you don't have to drink alcohol – you can still have a good time!

Rachel, Agony Aunt

How dangerous is glue sniffing?

From: daniel@~~speaksafamily~~.com
To: steve.agonyuncle@~~agonyuncle~~.com
Date: Wednesday, October 14
Subject: Sniffing aerosols

Dear Steve

I know I've done something stupid, but now I'm really worried that I'm going to get sick. Last week me and my mates sniffed some spray from an aerosol we found in my dad's garage. At first I felt dizzy but then I threw up and we all had really sore eyes and throats afterwards. Then I heard that sniffing stuff like that can kill you. Now one of my friends wants to do it again. He says it's better than taking drugs, but is it really dangerous? I wish I'd never done it.

Daniel (14)

From: steve.agonyuncle@~~agonyuncle~~.com
To: daniel@~~speaksafamily~~.com
Date: Wednesday, October 14
Subject: Re: Sniffing aerosols

Dear Daniel

It sounds as if you have had a lucky escape. Sniffing any kind of glue, solvent, paint, lighter fuel or gas is extremely dangerous, and I'm not just saying that to frighten you! Many users die the first time they do it.

The chemicals in these things are really poisonous. They can cause your heart to stop or your throat to swell so that you can't breathe. The reason why some people do it is because they think they'll just feel a bit dizzy and light-headed, but what about when they choke on their own vomit or fall over and knock themselves out?

Tell your friends it is dangerous. If they decide to do it again, tell an adult.

Steve, Agony Uncle

The Facts

Solvent abuse

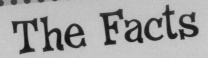 Solvent abuse means sniffing any kind of chemical or gas from an aerosol, paint, glue, lighter fuel, paint thinner or nail varnish remover.

One in four people who die from sniffing solvents are first-time users.

Sniffing solvents can cause hallucinations, which means seeing things that are not really there. This can lead to nasty accidents like falling down stairs.

People who sniff solvents are often unaware that the chemicals may cause heart failure, suffocation, or permanent damage to the brain, kidneys and liver.

Unlike smoking and drugs such as crack and alcohol, you cannot become physically addicted to solvents.

Your Views

Do you think it was too easy for Daniel to get hold of chemicals to sniff?

Is enough being done to make people aware of the dangers?

Glossary and websites

Acne persistent zits or pimples resulting from bacteria growing beneath blocked pores in the skin.

Addiction when your body becomes dependent on a drug such as alcohol or nicotine and finds it difficult to be without it.

Alcohol an addictive substance which dulls your senses and leads to a loss of control. It is found in drinks such as lager, wine, cider and spirits. Spirits such as vodka contain the highest concentration of alcohol.

Alcopops drinks with a strong alcoholic base mixed with sugar and fruit flavours.

Allergy a strong physical reaction to a substance like peanuts or a bee sting.

Anorexia a serious eating disorder. The sufferer does not eat enough to sustain a healthy body.

Asthma an inflammation of the airways, making it difficult to breathe.

Body odour (BO) occurs when bacteria feeds on the sweat in our armpits and groin area, producing a bad smell.

Diet what you eat and drink. A healthy diet includes plenty of fresh fruit and vegetables, protein (meat, eggs, fish, beans and lentils), carbohydrates (bread, pasta and rice), and not too much fat, sugar or salt.

Growth spurt when the body grows rapidly during puberty, normally for a period of 2 or 3 years. Boys often start their growth spurts later than girls.

Nicotine an addictive drug found in cigarettes.

Obese a medical term for someone who is dangerously overweight.

Periods during puberty, a girl's uterus, or womb, develops a lining of blood and tissue in preparation for pregnancy. This lining is where a fertilized egg may implant itself after sexual intercourse. However, when there is no fertilized egg the lining comes away each month and passes out through the vagina as a few spoonfuls of menstrual blood.

Pregnancy may happen to a girl after sexual intercourse when sperm from a boy's penis joins with an egg from a girl's ovaries. If the fertilized egg implants itself into the lining of the girl's womb, she is pregnant and a baby embryo will develop.

Puberty when your body responds to chemical signals, or hormones, and you begin to grow rapidly. Your sex organs develop in preparation for parenthood. Girls develop breasts, pubic and underarm hair and their periods start. Boys develop a larger penis and testicles, their voices drop and they grow pubic and underarm hair. Hormones in your body may also affect your emotions.

Sex organs in girls, ovaries (producing eggs) and uterus, or womb. In boys, testicles (producing sperm) and penis.

Solvent abuse sniffing any kind of chemical or gas from an aerosol, paint, glue, lighter fuel, paint thinner or nail varnish remover. Often called 'glue-sniffing', it is very dangerous.

Note to parents and teachers: Every effort has been made by the Publishers to ensure that these websites are suitable for children, that they are of the highest educational value, and that they contain no inappropriate or offensive material. However, because of the nature of the Internet, it is impossible to guarantee that the contents of these sites will not be altered. We strongly advise that Internet access is supervised by a responsible adult.

UK

www.lifebytes.gov.uk
Information on a variety of health matters including puberty, diet, smoking, drugs and alcohol.

www.childrenfirst.nhs.uk
An interactive site dealing with a wide range of life and health issues.

www.bbc.co.uk/health/kids
Useful information on subjects such as smoking, alcohol and healthy eating.

www.childline.org.uk
Has a fact sheet on eating disorders.

www.edauk.com
Information and advice on anorexia and other eating disorders.

www.nutrition.org.uk
Contains facts about a balanced diet.

www.asthma.org.uk/kidszone
Easy-to-use site for kids with asthma.

www.surgerydoor.co.uk
Go to 'Alcohol' and then 'Facts for young people' for clear advice.

www.roycastle.org/kats
Site of the Lung Cancer Foundation, with facts on smoking and health.

AUSTRALIA

www.cyh.com.au
Really useful information on puberty.

www.healthstar.com.au
Information, quizzes and games on a range of health issues.

www.allergyfacts.org.au
'Kids Corner' uses animal characters to explain different types of allergies.

Index

First published in 2005 by Franklin Watts
96 Leonard Street, London EC2A 4XD

Franklin Watts Australia
45-51 Huntley Street
Alexandria, NSW 2015

© Franklin Watts 2005

Series editor: Sarah Peutrill
Art director: Jonathan Hair
Design: Rita Storey
Picture researcher: Diana Morris
Advisor: Wendy Anthony, Health
education consultant

ISBN 0 7496 6045 7

Printed in Hong Kong/China

Picture credits: Paul Baldesare/Photofusion: 11,
13. Yves de Beugher/Alamy: 19. Jackie
Chapman/Photofusion/Alamy: 12. Bob
Daemmrich/Image Works/Topham: 14b. DPPI/Rex
Features: 23. Richard Gardner/Rex Features: 24.
Gina Glover/Photofusion: front cover b, 3, 16.
Brian Harris/Rex Features: 20. Ute
Klaphake/Photofusion: front cover t, 18b. Richard
Lord/Image Works/Topham: 9. Ray Moller/Watts:
14t, 18t. John Powell/Rex Features: 25. Ulrike
Preuss/Photofusion: 7. Nancy Richmond/Image
Works/Topham: 10, 22. Ellen Sensi/Image
Works/Topham: 15, 17t. Christa
Stadtler/Photofusion: 26. Bill Truslow/Rex Features:
6. Voisin/Phanie/Rex Features: 8. Watts: 21. Jennie
Woodcock/Reflections/Corbis: 27.

Every attempt has been made to clear copyright.
Should there be any inadvertent omission please
apply to the publisher for rectification.